D1307914

Marie Curie

History Maker Bios

Laura Hamilton Waxman

LERNER PUBLICATIONS COMPANY • MINNEAPOLIS

For my mom, Anita Waxman, who by example inspires me to be the best person I can be

The author wishes to thank Professor Monwhea Jeng of the Physics Department at Southern Illinois University in Edwardsville for his help with the preparation of this book.

Illustrations by Tim Parlin

Lerner Publications Company
A division of Lerner Publishing Group
241 First Avenue North
Minneapolis, MN 55401 U.S.A.

Website address: www.lernerbooks.com

Library of Congress Cataloging-in-Publication Data

Waxman, Laura Hamilton.
    Marie Curie / by Laura Hamilton Waxman.
        p.   cm. — (History maker bios)
    Includes bibliographical references and index.
    ISBN: 0–8225–0300–X (lib. bdg. : alk. paper)
    1. Curie, Marie, 1867–1934. 2. Chemists—Poland—Biography. [1. Curie, Marie, 1867–1934. 2. Chemists. 3. Scientists. 4. Women—Biography.] I. Title. II. Series.
    QD22.C8W38 2004
    540'.92—dc21   2002154872

Manufactured in the United States of America
1 2 3 4 5 6 – DP – 09 08 07 06 05 04

TABLE OF CONTENTS

INTRODUCTION

Women in the early 1900s could be wives and mothers. They could be teachers or tutors. But they were not supposed to be scientists or professors. Marie Curie never let those ideas stop her. She made up her mind that she would be a scientist. She devoted her life to the study of radioactivity.

Marie Curie was the first woman to win the Nobel Prize and the first person ever to win it twice. Her work on radioactivity helped scientists understand the world better. It helped doctors cure cancer. And it helped to change the way people thought about women. But Marie did not set out to change the world. She simply followed her dream—to be the best scientist she could be.

This is her story.

1 A Scientist Is Born

Maria Sklodowska was born on November 7, 1867, to a family who loved to learn. They called her Manya. Manya's parents were teachers in Warsaw, Poland. Her mother, Bronislawa, was headmistress at the best girls' school in the city. Her father, Vladislav, taught high school math and science. They taught Manya, her brother, and her three sisters to think for themselves.

Learning in the Sklodowski home was loud and messy. To teach the family history, Manya's father had his children make paper collages. To teach geography, he invented a noisy game using wooden blocks. To teach his children to be strong, he led nightly exercises before bed. He was always willing to answer any question that popped into his children's heads. To Manya, he was as good as any encyclopedia or dictionary.

At the age of three, Manya (CENTER) poses with her sisters and brother (LEFT TO RIGHT): Zosia, Hela, Jozio, and Bronya.

By the time Manya started school, she could already read. She quickly became the best student in her class. With her light, curly hair and her pale gray eyes, she looked like any other Polish girl. But her classmates knew she was special. Manya had an amazing ability to remember facts. At home, her brother and sisters would make a game of trying to distract her from her studies. But none of their tricks worked.

LAWBREAKERS

Once a week, Manya and her family broke the law. On Saturday nights, the Sklodowkis listened to Vladislav read Polish poetry. Russian czars had ruled Poland for more than one hundred years. The czar, the leader of Russia, had forbidden reading anything written in Polish. Manya's parents knew they could be punished for breaking the law whenever they taught their children Polish history or folktales. But they wanted their children to be proud of their homeland.

Manya's high school diploma

In 1873, Manya's father lost his teaching job. To make ends meet, he opened a boarding school in the Sklodowskis' home. The house was always overcrowded and noisy. At night, Manya slept on a couch to make room for the extra people. After school, she searched out a quiet corner of the house to study. Still, she managed to keep up with her schoolwork.

When Manya was ten, her mother died of an illness called tuberculosis. For Manya, the loss was almost too hard to bear. She threw herself into her studies. When she was fifteen, she graduated from high school at the top of her class.

Manya, Bronya, and Hela
(LEFT TO RIGHT.) with their
father in 1890. Bronya was
home from Paris for a visit.

Manya would have
loved to go to the
university in Warsaw, but that was out of
the question. Only men were allowed to go
there. The few women who did study at a
university often went to the Sorbonne in
Paris, France.

Manya's older sister, Bronya, wanted to
study medicine at the Sorbonne. She had
just enough savings to get to Paris. Manya
promised to find work and send money to
her sister. That way Bronya could study to
become a doctor. After that, Bronya would
pay for Manya's schooling in Paris.

Manya worked as a teacher in northern Poland to earn the needed money. At night, she studied on her own. She read thick books on everything from history to chemistry to math. During these lonely nights, she discovered a love for science. She read everything she could on physics, the study of energy and matter. She learned about matter, the substance that makes up all things.

After six years in Paris, Bronya wrote to Manya. She had finished her studies and become a doctor. Manya was ready to join her sister. She knew exactly what she was going to do in Paris. She was going to become a scientist.

2 FROM MANYA TO MARIE

Manya left Warsaw for Paris in 1891. At first she lived with Bronya and her new husband, Casimir Dluski. But as soon as she could, Manya found a small apartment of her own. In the winter, her apartment was bitterly cold. She had to sleep with all of her blankets and clothing piled on top of her just to stay warm.

The apartment was just a short walk from the Sorbonne. Manya always left for her classes a little earlier than she needed to. She wanted to be there in time to get a seat in the front row. She listened carefully to every word of each lecture. And she took careful notes as her professors wrote on the chalkboard.

Manya walked through the streets of Paris from her apartment to the laboratory.

Manya was too intent on her studies to pay attention to her place in the school. Still, she knew she was different. To fit in better, she changed her name from the Polish *Manya* to the French *Marie.* But she could not change the fact that she stood out as a woman. All of her professors and nearly all of the other students were men. The few female students were often teased.

Even so, Marie was happy with her new life. She took classes in physics and math. In the warm, gas-lit library, she got lost in her equations. "Work gives life the sweet taste of happiness," Marie wrote.

FREEDOM IN FRANCE

Marie was so happy to be in Paris that she ignored her hardships as a poor student. Warsaw had been strictly ruled by Russia. But Paris was known as a center of free thought. The city drew some of the world's greatest artists, writers, and scholars. Like Marie, these people thrived on the freedom of being able to think and do as they pleased.

Marie was looking for laboratory space when she met Pierre Curie. A friend thought that Pierre, who taught at a science school, might be able to find room at the school for Marie.

After three years of hard work, she graduated near the top of her class with a degree in physics. Then she began to study for a degree in math.

In the spring of 1894, Marie met a scientist named Pierre Curie. Right away, she noticed his gentle manner, handsome face, and clear brown eyes. Marie discovered that she and Pierre shared a great love of science.

It did not take long for Pierre to fall in love with Marie. He wanted her to marry him. That would mean staying in France for good. Marie loved her family and her homeland. But she had come to love Pierre as well. They had the same dream. Together, they promised, they would share a life of science.

Pierre and Marie shared a passion for science. At the time, they were both studying magnetism.

3 THOSE MYSTERIOUS RAYS

Marie and Pierre were married on July 26, 1895. Marie was twenty-seven, and Pierre was thirty-six. Always practical, Marie wore a blue dress for her wedding. Chemical stains wouldn't show on a dark dress, so she could wear it later in the laboratory.

Marie learned how to cook from her sister Bronya. But Pierre had not married Marie for her cooking skills. Pierre and Marie were happiest when they could discuss electricity or magnetism together.

In the fall of 1897, the Curies had something else to be happy about. Marie gave birth to a baby girl. The Curies named her Irène. Marie started a notebook. It was filled with facts about the baby—her weight, the size of her head, the food she ate. Marie even recorded the first sounds Irène made, "gogli, gogli, go."

For their honeymoon, Pierre and Marie toured France on their bicycles.

Roentgen's X-ray photograph of his wife's hand. His amazing discovery caught the attention of people around the world.

Marie still yearned to become a scientist. She had been reading about the work of a German scientist named Wilhelm Roentgen. Roentgen had discovered some mysterious rays. They were not bright, like rays of light. But they were much more powerful. They could pass through wood and skin and muscle. He called them X rays. With X rays, he took a photograph of the bones in his wife's hand.

A French scientist named Henri Becquerel discovered a weaker kind of ray. Becquerel's rays could not go through skin, but they could go through thick paper.

Becquerel's rays fascinated Marie. She wanted to learn everything she could about them. Becquerel had discovered that the rays were given off by an element called uranium. Marie knew that elements were the basic substances that made up all other materials in the universe. Gold, lead, and oxygen were well-known elements.

In a small laboratory, Marie began to test uranium. She hoped to learn how it produced Becquerel's rays. The days flew by as she did one experiment after the next.

Becquerel's rays made this dark spot on a photographic plate.

After a while, Marie had a new idea. Maybe other elements also produced these mysterious rays. This idea was thrilling. She decided to test every kind of matter she could find and compare it to uranium. It would take time, but Marie was patient.

THE FORGETFUL CURIES

Marie and Pierre had the same ability to focus completely on their work. Often, the day would pass before they realized that they had not eaten. When they did remember to sit down for a meal, they talked about their work. Sometimes they became so caught up in their conversation that they forgot all about the food in front of them. "You must sit down in peace before your meals and swallow them slowly," a worried friend told them. "You must not read or talk physics while you eat." It was good advice. But Marie and Pierre were too stubborn to follow it.

Pierre often joined his wife in her work. The Curies wrote down their findings and ideas in their shared notebook. They took their work very seriously. But when the weather turned warm, they also took time away from Paris.

As a family, they spent several weeks at the beach on the coast of France. Other times they visited the Sklodowski family in Poland. But after several weeks away, both Marie and Pierre were eager to return to their laboratory.

Marie shared a lab notebook with Pierre. Pierre's writing is on the left. Marie's is on the right.

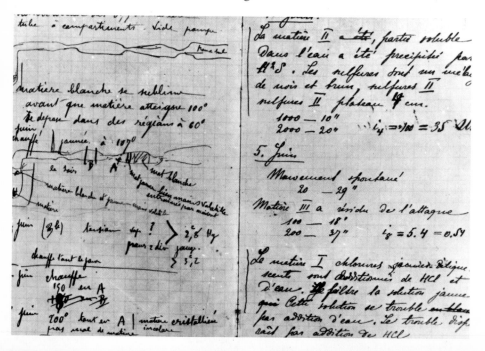

Marie works in her small basement laboratory. The room could be extremely cold. Rain leaked through the ceiling. But she was happy there.

One day in February 1898, Marie tested a material called pitchblende. Pitchblende contained a small amount of uranium. Marie guessed that the uranium in pitchblende would produce rays. She thought there wouldn't be many rays because there wasn't much uranium in pitchblende.

When Marie wrote down the results of her tests that day, she was sure she had made a mistake. The pitchblende did give off rays, as Marie expected. But there were many more rays than what uranium produced alone. She tested the pitchblende again and again with the same surprising results. How could this be? she wondered. Was there an unknown element in pitchblende that also produced rays? Marie set out to find the answer.

4 NEW ELEMENTS

Marie and Pierre worked together from winter into summer and through the next winter. Day after day, they tried to find the unknown element in pitchblende. They tested it again and again.

Late in 1898, they made an amazing discovery. They found not one, but two new elements in pitchblende.

In their dark laboratory, Marie and Pierre loved to watch the light coming from the radium.

Marie decided to name the first element *polonium*, in honor of Poland. She named the second element *radium*, after the Latin word for ray. Radium gave off the strongest rays of all. These rays glowed in the dark with a magical blue light.

Marie invented a new word for elements that produced rays. She called them *radioactive* elements.

The Curies knew they had discovered two new elements. But they did not have proof. To prove the elements existed, they would have to separate out pure polonium and pure radium from the pitchblende.

Marie decided to devote herself first to separating out the radium. She needed huge amounts of water and chemicals. She needed several tons of pitchblende. And she needed time. Marie would have to spend years boiling the pitchblende in the water and chemicals. That would allow her to break down the pitchblende. If she was successful, she would end up with a tiny amount of pure radium.

Pierre and his brother Jacques invented this device to measure electrical current. Marie needed the device for her work with radium.

Marie and Pierre moved into a larger laboratory. It was a wooden shed with a glass ceiling that did not keep out the rain. It was cold and nearly empty. Inside were just a few old wooden tables, a poorly working cast-iron stove, and one blackboard. Still, it was better than what they had before.

In their new laboratory, Pierre and Marie worked on separating pure elements from pitchblende.

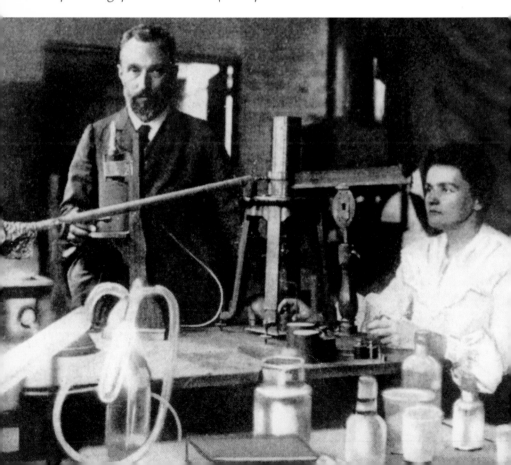

Marie (BACK ROW, CENTER) with her students at a teachers' college

In 1900, the Curies moved to a two-story house just outside of Paris. Pierre's father lived with them. The house had lots of sunlight and a lovely garden. These were the things that Marie cared about most. She didn't bother with fancy furniture or carpets.

To help pay for the house, Marie found a job at a teacher's college. The college prepared women to become schoolteachers. Marie was the first female teacher in the college. She was also the first person to teach the students physics.

Each day Marie traveled into the city to work in her laboratory and teach her classes. In the evening, Marie returned home to be with her daughter. But sometimes the pull of her work was too strong. After Irène was asleep, Marie and Pierre would quietly leave their daughter with Pierre's father and go back to the laboratory.

Marie and Pierre sit in their garden with six-year-old Irène.

The Curies' Nobel Prize for physics. These highly respected prizes are presented once each year to scientists, writers, doctors, economists, and peacemakers who have done extraordinary work.

In 1903, Marie and Pierre received a great honor. The two of them, along with Henri Becquerel, won the Nobel Prize in physics. This award was one of the most respected awards in the world. The prize honored the Curies and Becquerel for their groundbreaking work on radioactivity. Never before had it been given to a woman, or to a husband-and-wife team.

Suddenly the quiet and private Marie was pushed into the spotlight. Everyone wanted to know about the female scientist, Madame Curie. Her discovery of radium made her famous. Doctors learned that radiation, the rays given off by radium, could help cure deadly cancers. Radiation might cure arthritis and even mental illnesses. Marie was delighted to know that her work would help people. But she disliked all the attention.

CURIE CRAZINESS

After Marie won the Nobel Prize, reporters and photographers burst into her life. They wanted to know everything about her. When Marie refused to be interviewed, reporters wrote about her daughter, her daughter's nanny, even her black-and-white cat. Marie received piles of mail from all over the world. People sent her poems about radium. One man wrote to ask if he could name his racehorse Marie in her honor.

Pierre teaching at the Sorbonne

Reporters and photographers constantly tried to see her. "One would like to dig into the ground somewhere to find a little peace," she wrote to a relative in Poland.

Something good did come out of all the fuss. Pierre was hired as a professor at the Sorbonne. The university would not consider hiring a woman as a professor. Instead, Pierre hired Marie as the chief of his laboratory at the Sorbonne.

5 MADAME CURIE

At the end of 1904, Marie began a new notebook. It was for a new baby, Ève. The baby brought great joy to Marie's already happy life. She and Pierre continued their research on radioactivity. And Pierre was elected into the French Academy of Sciences.

But on April 19, 1906, Marie's happiness vanished. It was a rainy day in Paris. As Pierre crossed a narrow street, he was run over by a horse-drawn carriage. He died immediately.

Marie could not begin to imagine living without Pierre. He had been her partner in every way. His gentle support and love had meant everything to her. He had helped her to be the best mother, wife, and scientist she could be.

Marie with eight-year-old Irène and one-year-old Ève. She raised the girls in the same way that her parents had raised her.

At first Marie would not even think of continuing her work on radioactivity. She didn't want to return to the laboratory. Everything there reminded her of Pierre and the life they had shared. But as days and weeks passed, she felt a gentle pull. Her work was tugging at her once again.

Slowly, Marie returned to her research and her beloved laboratory. There she could block out the world around her. She could focus all of her thoughts on the miracle of the glowing rays.

Marie finally returned to her laboratory and her work in the new science of radioactivity.

Scientists gather at the first international physics conference. Marie bends over to puzzle something out with two other scientists. (Albert Einstein is second from the right.)

Marie was offered Pierre's teaching job at the Sorbonne. She was the first female professor ever to teach there. On the afternoon of her first class, hundreds of people filled up the lecture hall to hear her speak. Her students were there. So were reporters and people who simply wanted to see the famous Madame Curie.

Marie Curie and Albert Einstein talk as they hike.

Marie was busier than ever. But each day she took the train home to have lunch with her daughters. She was greatly involved in her daughters' schooling. And she encouraged Irène and Ève to follow their interests.

As a famous scientist, Marie met other famous scientists. She formed a warm friendship with Albert Einstein. Marie and Albert loved to discuss physics and politics. One year, the Curie and Einstein families went on a hiking trip together. While the children played, Marie and Albert spent hours talking.

Marie's laboratory became a place where scientists from all over the world came to study radioactivity. They also studied cancer and its treatment. Marie continued her research with polonium and radium. By 1910, she finally separated out pure amounts of each of the elements. There was no doubt that she had discovered two new elements.

CURIETHERAPY

Doctors believed the rays from radium had great healing powers. Radium treatments, also called curietherapy, soon became all the rage. Doctors used radium to treat diseases such as cancer, lupus, and gout. They also used it on birthmarks, ulcers, and certain mental illnesses. Patients could breathe radium fumes, swallow radium liquid, have a radium bath, or receive a radium shot. Years later, scientists learned that exposure to large amounts of radium can be deadly. Radium is still used to cure cancer, but it is used in much smaller doses than it was in Marie's time.

One year later, Marie received some surprising news. She was awarded a second Nobel Prize. This time she won the prize in chemistry for the discovery of radium and polonium. She was the first person ever to win two Nobel prizes.

World War I broke out in Eastern Europe in 1914. Soon all of Europe was involved. Marie knew she had to help France during the war. She was shocked to discover that few army hospitals had X-ray machines.

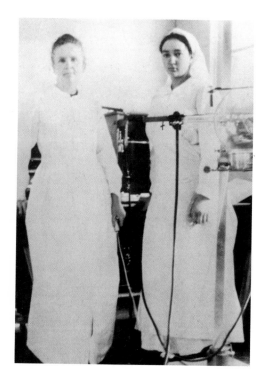

These new machines allowed doctors to see exactly where a soldier was injured.

Marie and Irène with X-ray equipment at a military hospital. Marie trained Irène to set up X-ray machines on a battlefront on her own.

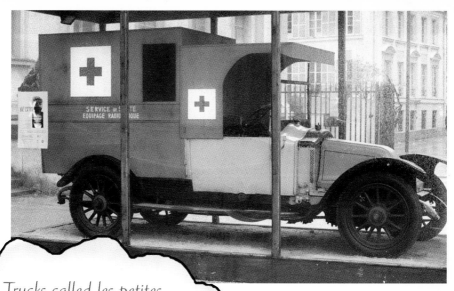

Trucks called *les petites Curies* brought X-ray equipment to battlefronts in World War I.

There were not enough X-ray machines to go around. But Marie had an idea. She found sturdy trucks that could hold X-ray equipment. The trucks could go from one army hospital to the next. This gave many doctors a chance to use the machines on their patients. These trucks became known as *les petites Curies*, or "the little Curies," in French.

Marie trained people to use the X-ray machines on the petites Curies. Seventeen-year-old Irène helped her mother. Their hard work saved the lives of many soldiers.

Although Marie did not know it, she was suffering from radium sickness. This kind of sickness comes to people who are exposed to large amounts of radium.

The war ended in 1918, and Marie returned to her laboratory. It was now called the Radium Institute. There she worked with Irène and dozens of other scientists. The institute became famous all over the world.

As Marie grew older, her health began to fail. Over the years, she had been exposed to too much radium, and it had made her sick. Marie died on July 4, 1934, at the age of sixty-six.

The researchers who came after Marie built on her work. Irène won the Nobel Prize in 1935 for her work on radioactivity. Other scientists learned from Marie's example. Time and time again, Marie had struggled to find an answer to a question or a solution to a problem. Never once did she give up. She proved she was the best scientist she could be.

TIMELINE

In the year . . .

1873 Marie's father lost his teaching job and opened up a boarding school.

1878 her mother died on May 9.   `Age 10`

1891 she began her studies at the Sorbonne.

1895 She married Pierre Curie on July 26.   `Age 27`

1897 her daughter Irène was born.

1898 she first used the term radioactivity on April 12.
she and Pierre announced the discoveries of polonium and radium in July and December.

1903 she and Pierre won the Nobel Prize for physics, along with Henri Becquerel.   `Age 36`

1904 her daughter Ève was born.

1906 Pierre Curie died on April 19.
she became the first female professor at the Sorbonne.

1911 she won the Nobel Prize in chemistry.   `Age 44`

1914 the Radium Institute was built.
World War I began.

1918 World War I ended.

1921 she traveled to the United States in May and June.

1934 she died on July 4.   `Age 66`

44

WHAT IS AN ATOM?

When Marie first began studying radioactivity, scientists knew about the tiny particles called atoms. Atoms make up everything around us, from air to wood to water. Atoms are too small to see, even with the most powerful microscope. A speck of dust is made of billions and billions of atoms.

For many years, scientists believed that atoms were the smallest part of any material. Marie's work helped change that. She guessed that the rays coming from radioactive elements were produced by the atoms that made up those elements. She believed the atoms themselves were radioactive. This new idea helped other scientists discover something amazing about atoms. Tiny atoms are actually made up of even smaller parts. These parts are called electrons, protons, and neutrons. Some radioactive atoms give off energy, while others give off some of the tiny particles of which they are made.

FURTHER READING

NONFICTION

Fox, Karen. *The Chain Reaction: Pioneers of Nuclear Science.* New York: Franklin Watts, 1998. Profiles seven men and women whose studies of the atom changed the world.

Kahn, Jetty. *Women in Chemistry Careers.* Mankato, MN: Capstone, 2000. Explores the life work of female scientists, inventors, and aviators.

McClafferty, Carla Killough. *The Head Bone's Connected to the Neck Bone: The Weird, Wacky, and Wonderful X-Ray.* New York: Farrar, Straus, and Giroux, 2001. Outlines the history of the X ray from Roentgen's discovery to its present-day uses in medicine and industry.

McPherson, Stephanie Sammartino. *Albert Einstein.* Minneapolis: Lerner Publications, 2004. A biography of the scientist who discovered relativity.

FICTION

Zonta, Pat. *Jessica's X-Ray.* Toronto: Firefly Books, 2002. Jessica breaks her arm and learns how X rays work. Includes a tour of the radiology department and photographs of X rays, MRI scans, and ultrasounds.

WEBSITES

Access Excellence: The National Health Museum—The Discovery of Radioactivity
<http://www.accessexcellence.org/AE/AEC/CC /radioactivity.html> This site shows the history of our understanding of the atom. Includes activities.

Marie Curie and the Science of Radioactivity
<http://www.aip.org/history/curie/> An excellent site outlining Marie Curie's life and her contributions to science.

Nobel E-Museum
<http://www.nobel.se/> All about the Nobel Prize, including information on all of the winners for each award: physics, chemistry, medicine, literature, economics, and peace.

SELECT BIBLIOGRAPHY

Curie, Ève. *Madame Curie: A Biography by Ève Curie*. New York: Doubleday, 1937.

Pasachoff, Naomi. *Marie Curie and the Science of Radioactivity*. New York: Oxford University Press, 1996.

Pflaum, Rosalynd. *Grand Obsession: Marie Curie and Her World*. New York: Doubleday, 1989.

Quinn, Susan. *Marie Curie: A Life*. New York: Simon & Schuster, 1995.

INDEX

Acknowledgments

For photographs and artwork: AIP Emilio Segrè Visual Archives, pp. 4, 15, 18, 19, 30, 38; ACJC-Curie and Joliot-Curie fund, pp. 7, 9, 10, 20, 22, 26, 27, 29, 31, 33, 40; Hulton/Archive by Getty Images, pp. 13, 16; Radium Institute, courtesy AIP Emilio Segrè Visual Archives, p. 23; AIP Emilio Segrè Visual Archives, E. Scott Barr Collection, p. 28; © Bettmann/CORBIS, pp. 35, 36; Photographie Benjamin Couprie, Institut International de Physique Solvay, courtesy AIP Emilio Segrè Visual Archives, p. 37; © Jay Pasachoff, p. 41; Library of Congress, p. 42.
Front cover, A. M. Chesney Medical Archives, John Hopkins Medical Institute, courtesy AIP Emilio Segrè Visual Archives.
Back cover, ACJC-Curie and Joliot-Curie fund.
For quoted material: pp. 14, 18, 33, Susan Quinn, *Marie Curie: A Life* (New York: Simon & Schuster, 1995); p. 20, Ève Curie, *Madame Curie: A Biography by Ève Curie* (New York: Doubleday, 1937).